WHAT DAY OF THE WEEK WAS CHRIST CRUCIFIED?

FRIDAY?
THURSDAY?
WEDNESDAY?

A Brief Study of Scripture

By

Dr. Bob C Green

June 2021

REL006201: Religion: Biblical Studies - Topical

ISBN 978-1-7371005-5-3

All Scripture quotes are from the King James Bible.

Address All Inquiries To:
THE OLD PATHS PUBLICATIONS, Inc.
142 Gold Flume Way
Cleveland, Georgia, U.S.A.

Web: www.theoldpathspublications.com
E-mail: TOP@theoldpathspublications.com

1.0

PREFACE

As a young preacher, I often struggled with certain inconsistencies that I had found in the teachings that I had received at church. Please do not misunderstand. I am grateful for all of the positive and correct teachings that I received as a child and teenage preacher. Due to the godly influence of my parents and the sound preaching of the Bible by our pastors, the Lord saved me at a very early age, called me into the ministry of His Word, and instilled in my heart a love for HIM, for the Bible and for the Holy Spirit.

One of the matters that concerned me was the fact that most mainline churches, including ours, taught their members to believe that Christ had died on "Good Friday." Though I must admit that my knowledge of the Scripture was very limited, I could not reconcile this teaching with what I read in the Bible. I am grateful to the Lord for having established my faith in His Holy Word. In my heart I knew that if there was a problem, it was not with the Word of God.

My young faith was strengthened and I was definitely encouraged when I heard a scholarly Biblical explanation of the facts related to Christ's death, burial and resurrection. It thrilled my heart to realize that there was someone with sufficient knowledge of the Old and New Testament Scripture to present an accurate account of the Lord's death, burial and resurrection. I was challenged to a more thorough study of the Bible by the teaching of Evangelist Ed Vallowe. A portion of what will be presented from the Scripture in this study was gleaned from Dr. Vallowe's exposition of the Bible.

Though I have been greatly blessed in the past fifty-three years as HE has graciously allowed me to minister His

Word, I have also been blessed by the constant discovery of truth that has come by continual study of the Bible. The Holy Spirit has opened my understanding to so much truth that needed to be applied and practiced in my life. The most important fact in this hour is that "Christ died for our sins according to the Scripture, that he was buried, and that he rose again the third day... in order to provide the greatest need and the greatest blessing to mankind, eternal salvation.

Jesus died for you and for me. HE lives today. Do you know Him?

TABLE OF CONTENTS

THE QUESTION

ACCORDING TO THE SCRIPTURE, ON WHICH DAY OF THE WEEK WAS OUR LORD JESUS CHRIST CRUCIFIED AND BURIED?   ON WHICH DAY OF THE WEEK DID HE COME FORTH FROM THE GRAVE?

Many non-believers attempt to discredit the Scriptures using the confusion about which days of the week were involved in the death, burial, and resurrection of the Lord Jesus Christ. It is critical that we use the Bible to correct the erroneous teachings and traditions that have resulted from inaccurate interpretation of the Scriptures.   Please understand that I recognize that many of those that have accepted the traditions taught concerning His death, burial and resurrection are indeed sincere believers.

What the Bible teaches about the death, burial and resurrection of Christ is foundational to our Christian faith and practice. It is also the foundation for our salvation. The Bible as God's holy, divinely inspired and preserved Word is a "precise" book, and every word is faithful and true. There is grave danger when the "traditions of men" supplant or negate the Word of God.   The Lord warned His disciples of this problem. Any time there is a difference between what the Bible says and what is taught by the "tradition of men", the Bible should be believed and followed. Bible truth does not contradict Bible truth.

What seems to be a contradiction can often be resolved by simply "comparing Scripture with Scripture."   The teaching that Christ died on Friday is an example of "religious tradition" contradicting Scripture. If Christ were to remain in the tomb three days and three nights, as He said (Matthew

12:40), how could He possibly have died on Friday before resurrection Sunday?

In our study we will deal with the strongest argument presented in favor of His death on Friday. This is found in John 19:31 and will be explained in good time.

Biblically, the Lord Jesus Christ died on what we call Wednesday. Before dismissing this statement please take time to review the study of this little booklet; comparing Scripture with Scripture. For centuries it has been taught that Christ died on Friday. The main line denominations of Christianity have accepted this teaching which has roots in the traditions of Rome. It is strange that in many other issues it is demanded that the teachings be clear and consistent, but in this matter many have been willing to accept a teaching that in reality contradicts the very words of the Savior. Let us begin by considering the following verses:

*"Moreover, brethren, I declare unto you **the gospel** which I preached unto you, which also ye have received, and wherein ye stand; By which also ye are saved, if ye keep in memory what I preached unto you, unless ye have believed in vain. For I delivered unto you first of all that which I also received, how that **Christ died for our sins according to the scriptures;** And **that he was buried**, and that **he rose again the third day according to the scriptures:** And that he was seen of Cephas,..."* I Corinthians 15:1-5a

*"...For as Jonas was **three days and three nights** in the whale's belly; so shall the Son of man be three days and three nights in the heart of the earth."* Matthew 12:40

In the first few verses of I Corinthians 15, the Apostle Paul says that that Christ died according to the Scripture, that he was buried and that he rose again according to the Scripture. It is for us to know just what the Scriptures say concerning his death, his burial and his resurrection. It should be remembered that the "Scriptures" to which Paul referred were the Scriptures of the Old Testament. The New Testament did not exist as of yet or might we say, "it was being written."

A. JESUS AND JONAH AND THE SCRIPTURES…

In Matthew 12:40 the Lord Jesus says to his disciples that he would be **three days and three nights** in the heart of the earth. If Jesus had intended to say three days or only a portion of three days and one night, that is what he would have said. It is not difficult to believe that Jesus always said what he meant and meant what he said.

It is interesting to note that **Jesus** in the process of stating how long he would be in the tomb **confirms the validity of Jonah and his experience in the belly of the whale.** If one denies the fact that Jonah was a prophet and that God had prepared a big fish to swallow him, he/she must also deny Jesus Christ. Jesus said Jonah was a prophet and used his experience in the belly of the whale to prefigure his own experience with death and the grave. Whoa be to the person who would suggest Jesus was deceived, delusional or just telling a bold faced lie. **If** Jesus had said Jonah swallowed a whale…We would be obligated to believe it, because He is the truth… John 14:6. With that said, let us proceed to see the significance of Jonah's experience.

Jonah had been commanded to preach repentance to the people of Nineveh. He rebelled against God and refused to preach, as a Hebrew, to the people of Nineveh, a gentile city. He attempted to flee from the presence of God by boarding a ship bound for Tarshish. The mariners soon realized that the Lord had sent a fierce storm because of Jonah's sin. The sailors feared for their lives and cast Jonah into the sea. The Bible then states that the "sea ceased from her raging" (Jonah 1:15). In verse 17 of Jonah Chapter One it is also stated, "…the Lord had prepared great fish to swallow up Jonah."

Jonah finally accepted God's will and prayed. The whale "vomited out Jonah upon the dry land." He ultimately went and preached to the people of Nineveh. They repented and God withheld judgment.

In Matthew 12:38 we are told that, "certain of the scribes and Pharisees answered, saying, Master, we would see a sign from thee." Jesus responded to their demand for a sign by saying that the only sign that would be given was "the sign of Jonah the prophet."

> *"For as Jonas was three days and three nights in the whale's belly; so shall **the Son of man be three days and three nights in the heart of the earth."*** Matthew 12:40

Three days and three nights would add up to seventy-two hours total. Unless these words are "spiritualized" and given some fabricated meaning, Jesus must have been indicating that he expected to spend three periods of daylight of 12 hours each and three periods of darkness, also 12 hours each. Three (days) plus three (nights) equals six. Six times 12 (hrs) equals seventy-two. The word "day" that is used by the Lord is used in other passages to refer to the hours of daylight of a day. The word "night" is used elsewhere to refer to the hours of darkness. According to the Lord, Jonah spent three days and three nights, or a total of seventy-two hours in the whale's belly. Since the Lord stated that he would spend three days and three nights in the heart of the earth, we can believe that he was to remain in the grave seventy-two hours.

To know when Christ died, we only have to subtract seventy-two hours from the time he came forth from the grave. We know from the testimony of Matthew that he was already risen "very early in the morning", because "it began to dawn toward the first day of the week" when Mary Magdalene and the other Mary went to see the sepulchre (Matthew 28:1). If Christ came forth from the tomb at 6:00 A.M. on Sunday morning then we subtract seventy-two hours from that moment. If he died Friday afternoon at 3:00 P.M., then we can figure this way:

TRADITIONAL THINKING	BIBLE TRUTH/JEWISH DAYS
Saturday night = 12 hours	Saturday (12 hrs of light, 12 hours of darkness = 24 hours
Saturday/day = 12 hours	Friday (12 hrs of light, 12 hours of darkness) = 24 hrs
Friday night = 12 hours	Thursday (12 hrs of light, 12 hours of darkness = 24 hrs
Friday/day = 3 hours	(This takes us back to Wednesday @ 6:00 PM)
A grand total of 39 hours	Total = 72 hrs

Following Traditional Thinking (see table) we lack 33 hours. According to Scripture (see table), we are right on target.

It is possible that Jesus did not really mean that he would be **three days _and_ three nights in the grave... really?**

B. OLD TESTAMENT TYPES, THE FEASTS OF THE LORD

Not only do we have the words of Jesus, we also have the "types" found in the Old Testament. The Passover Feast is one such type of Christ. Remember, a type is a figure or symbol of something. These types portrayed Christ in some way or fashion.

We must take into consideration that the only "Scripture" Paul had was the Scripture found in the Old Testament. When he stated in I Corinthians that Christ died, was buried and rose again according to the Scripture he must have been referring to the Scripture of the Old Testament. He, of course, could not be referring to the New Testament Scripture.

In the Old Testament book of Leviticus, chapter 23, we are given a list of the "feasts of the Lord" that were to be observed by Israel. The feasts are also called "holy convocations." God commanded Israel to do no "work" on those days.

> *Six days shall work be done: but the seventh day is the sabbath of rest,* ***an holy convocation****; ye shall do no work therein..."*
> Leviticus 23: 3

Please note that in verse three, the sabbath is called a holy convocation. This is important because this fact will contribute to the understanding that **there can be more than one "sabbath" in a week; more than just the seventh day sabbath or Saturday.**

A. The Passover is the **first** of the feasts of the Lord. It signaled the beginning of the Jewish religious year.

Keeping in mind the fact that a "type" prefigures the Lord or in some way represents Him or something of His life and ministry. We can say that the Passover is a "type of Christ's death." In John 1:29 we read that Jesus is the "Lamb of God." As such He gave himself, as the sacrificial Lamb of God, on the cross of Calvary. The sacrificial lamb of Exodus 12 prefigures the sacrifice of Christ. The lamb was spotless and without blemish. So too, Christ was the sinless Son of God. The lamb's blood was shed. The precious blood of Christ was also shed for our sins (Acts 20:28). Paul even calls Christ, "our Passover."

*"Purge out therefore the old leaven, that ye may be a new lump, as ye are unleavened, For even **Christ our Passover** is sacrificed for us:…"* I Corinthians 5:7

For some people the problem begins with the reference in John 19:31 to the Preparation Day and the sabbath, a high day.

"The Jews therefore, because it was the preparation, that the bodies should not remain upon the cross on the sabbath day, (**for that sabbath day was a high day**) *besought Pilate that their legs might be broken, and that they might be taken away."* John 19:31

The Passover was upon them. John 19:31 indicates that the Passover would begin the day after Jesus was crucified. The Jews wanted Pilate to have Jesus' legs and those of the two thieves broken in order to hasten their deaths. They wanted Jesus and the others to be taken down from the crosses before the beginning of the next day. The next day was identified as a "sabbath" or high and holy day. It would have been a violation of Jewish law to leave the bodies on the crosses on the Passover or special sabbath. It is clear from what John says in 19:31 that **Jesus was crucified on the cross on the Preparation Day before the sabbath, a high day.**

John 18:28 states that Jesus was taken, after his arrest in Gethsemane, from before Caiaphas and "led into the hall of judgment: and **it was early**; and they themselves [the Jews] went not into the judgment hall, lest they should be defiled; but that they might eat the Passover." Knowing that the Passover was upon them, the Jews wanted to be able to participate in it. They knew they would be defiled if they entered into the judgment hall or Praetorium on the Preparation Day. The Jews waited until:

> "...the next day, that followed the day of the preparation, the chief priests and Pharisees came together unto Pilate,..." Matthew 17:62

It is evident that the crucifixion of Jesus occurred on the **day before the "sabbath."** In order to answer the question, "When was Christ crucified?" we need to investigate and identify the "sabbath" mentioned in the passages quoted. Most people consider the sabbath mentioned to be the normal weekly Sabbath... in fact my computer wants to automatically change the "s" to a capital "S" every time I type the word Sabbath. Because most people interpret the words of John 19:31 to mean that Jesus died on the day before the weekly Sabbath or Saturday, they believe He must have been crucified on Friday.

If Christ was crucified on Friday, why does the general population call it "Good Friday"? What is "good" about sinful men killing the sinless Son of God? That Christ was crucified on Friday seems to be the obvious answer to the question of "when Christ died." This assumption seems reasonable until we realize that the Scriptures offer an alternative definition and identification of the term "sabbath."

The fact is that Scriptures teach that all seven days of the Passover were considered to be "High Days." In the Scriptures, the terms "Holy Days", "High Days" and the "sabbath" are used interchangeably. **In the Bible, there are days other than Saturday (Sabbath) considered to be "High Days" or "sabbaths." This very fact is indicated in Leviticus 16:29-31 and also 23:24-27.**

> *"And this shall be a statue for ever unto you: that in the seventh month on the tenth day of the month, ye shall afflict your souls, and do no work at all, whether it be one of your own country, or a stranger that sojourneth among you: For on that day shall the priest make an atonement for you, to cleanse you, that ye may be clean from all your sins before the LORD. It shall be a **sabbath** of rest unto you..."*
> Leviticus 16:29-31

> *"Speak unto the children of Israel, saying, In the seventh month, in the **first day of the month,** shall ye have a **sabbath,** a memorial of blowing the trumpets, an holy convocation. Ye shall **do no servile work** therein:... (Vs. 27) Also on **the tenth day** of the seventh month there shall be a day of atonement: it shall be an **holy convocation** unto you; ye shall afflict your souls, and offer an offering made by fire unto the LORD. Ye shall **do no work** in that same day: for it is a day of atonement for you before the LORD your God."*
> Leviticus 23:24, 27-28

15

In these verses in Leviticus, both the **first** and the **tenth** days of the seventh month were referred to as **"sabbaths or holy convocations"** (high days). Even John 19:31 confirms this point. Notice the phrase, **"that sabbath day was a high day",** indicating by the use of the article "a" – rather than the article "the" – that there may have been other days that were **"high days"** during that week besides the normal Sabbath (Saturday).

There is a parallel passage in Numbers 28:16-38. It should be noted in 28:16 the **Passover** was on the 14th of the month. In verses 17 the 15th is mentioned as the feast and instructions are given to observe seven days without "leaven" or the second feast, that of **Unleavened Bread**. In verse 18 they were told the first day of the feast would be a "holy convocation" and they were to do no work. This would have been a "sabbath." In verse 25, another holy convocation is ordered for the observance of the Feast of **Firstfruits**… again they were to do no work (vs. 26). In Leviticus 29:1, they were to set aside the 1st day of the 7th month for the Feast of **Trumpets**… it too was a holy convocation (a sabbath). In 29:7 they are told the "10th day" of the same month would be a holy convocation, the **Atonement**. Finally in 29:12, they were to observe the 15th day of the 7th month as a holy convocation, the Feast of **Tabernacles**. These additional verses confirm the fact that there were days of the week or month, other than the weekly Sabbath (Saturday) that were considered sabbaths.

   B. The **second** feast was that of the Unleavened Bread. During the days of this feast the Jews were to remove all leaven from their houses. Leaven is a "type" of sin. The removal of the leaven (sin), speaks to us of the death and burial of Jesus. By His death Christ paid the penalty of sin and removed it.

"But this man, after he had offered one sacrifice for sins for ever, sat down on the right hand of God." Hebrews 10:12

C. The **third** feast is that of the Firstfruits.

*"... When ye be come into the land which I give unto you, ye shall reap the harvest thereof, then ye shall bring a sheaf of the firstfruits of your harvest unto the priest: And ye shall wave the sheaf before the LORD, to be accepted for you: **on the morrow after the Sabbath** the priest shall wave it."* Leviticus 23:10-11

The offering of the firstfruits was to be made "on the morrow after the sabbath." The **firstfruits speak of the Lord Jesus Christ in His resurrection**... which surely occurred on the "morrow" after the weekly Sabbath (Saturday), on Sunday.

*"But now is Christ risen from the dead, and become the **firstfruits** of them that slept."* I Corinthians 15:20

D. The **fourth** feast is Pentecost. (Leviticus 23:15-22)

*"And ye shall count unto you from the morrow after the sabbath, from the day that ye brought the sheaf of the wave offering; seven sabbaths shall be complete: Even unto the **morrow after the seventh sabbath** shall ye number fifty days; and ye shall offer a new meat offering unto the LORD."*

The morrow (day) after the Sabbath would be a Sunday. Pentecost fell on Sunday and was the day on which the Holy

17

Spirit began to indwell the body of Christ. Christ's church grew from 120 to 3120 on that day .

E. The remaining feasts: **Trumpets, Atonement, and Tabernacles,** etc.

We will not take time to discuss these additional feasts of the LORD but go back to Leviticus 23.*Vss. 24, 27, 32.*

> *"… in the first day of the month, shall ye have a sabbath, a memorial of the blowing of trumpets, an holy convocation. … Also on the tenth day of this seventh month there shall be a day of atonement: it shall be a holy convocation unto you; and ye shall afflict your souls, and offer an offering made by fire unto the LORD. And ye shall do no work in that same day: for it is a day of atonement, to make atonement for you before the LORD your God. It shall be unto you a sabbath of rest, and ye shall afflict your souls: in the ninth day of the month at even, from even unto even, shall ye celebrate your sabbath."*

Please note the number of days that are referred to as sabbaths and holy convocations in these verses. It should also be noted that the first day of the month was called a sabbath as were the tenth day and the ninth day.

It **seems possible that Jesus could have been crucified on a day other than Friday** (the day before the normal weekly Sabbath), **because, according to the Scripture, there were other days of the week that were considered "sabbaths."** If the "first day of the seventh month was the weekly Sabbath (Saturday), then it reasons that the next weekly Sabbath (Saturday) would fall **eight days later**. But, the LORD says **the tenth day** of the seventh month was also a sabbath. Do not be distracted trying to figure out whether the first day of the seventh month was a Saturday. The point is that, according to Scriptures there was a ten day interval between the first sabbath and the additional declared sabbath on the tenth.

Without this information, it is easy for modern interpreters to make the mistake of saying that Christ died on Friday. Admittedly, if every **"sabbath"**, every **holy convocation,** or every **high day** was the weekly Sabbath or Saturday, then Christ was crucified for our sins on Friday. If that is the case then the confusion continues and the skeptics concerning the deity of Christ and the infallibility of the Scriptures seem justified.

Because Jesus Christ "died according to the Scripture" (I Corinthians 15:1-4) **and because Jesus Himself told His disciples the "He would be three days and three nights in the heart of the earth",** even as Jonah was an equal time in the belly of the great fish (Matthew 12:40), *JESUS COULD NOT HAVE DIED ON FRIDAY.* The Lord Jesus Christ said it. He never lies. His Word is true.

The fact there were other days of the week besides the weekly Sabbath that were considered sabbaths and because Jesus himself said that he would spend three days and three nights in the heart of the earth, are strong arguments in favor of Christ having died for our sins on a day other than a Friday. The "preparation" mentioned in John 19:31 did not necessarily have to be a Friday. John says the sabbath mentioned was a "high day" (vs. 31). John also records in John 20:1:

"The first day of the week (Sunday) cometh Mary Magdalene early, when it was yet dark,

unto the sepulchre, and seeth the stone taken away from the sepulchre."

Compare these words with those of Matthew who says,

"In the end of the sabbath, as it began to dawn toward the first day of the week, came Mary Magdalene..." Matthew 28:1.

These words leave no room for doubt concerning the fact that Jesus came forth from the grave "very early" on the first day of the week... on Sunday for sure. **There is no way to calculate "three days and three nights" between Friday afternoon and Sunday, "very early in the morning."** Even if we allow the few hours Friday afternoon to represent one day, Saturday to represent a second day and what might have been a few minutes Sunday to represent the third day, we do not have three nights.   If Christ died Friday afternoon, we only have Friday night and Saturday night. As will be explained later, we do not even have Friday night because the Jewish day began with 12 hours of darkness followed by 12 hours of daylight. What we call Friday night is actually Saturday night (12 hours of darkness)... but we'll save this point for later in the study.

The writer believes that the Biblical account of the **Passover** in Exodus, Chapter 12 sheds significant light on the issue as to when Jesus was actually crucified and placed in the tomb. This information can be added to the testimony of Scripture concerning the **experience of Jonah**

C. CHRIST, THE PASSOVER LAMB

As we study Exodus 12:3-6 we find the institution of the Jewish Passover. The Passover is a type of Jesus Christ. By "type" we mean a representation or a symbol or something that prefigures the Lord Jesus Christ. In verse three, the LORD orders Moses and Aaron to tell the congregation of Israel to take a lamb without spot or blemish on the **tenth day of the month** and to keep it shut away until the **fourteenth day of the same month.** The three days served to make certain that the lamb was indeed pure and worthy to be sacrificed. As a "type" the three days prefigure the three years of earthly ministry of the Lord Jesus Christ in which He proved Himself sinless and worthy to be offered as "the Lamb of God, which taketh away the sin of the world." (John 1:29, 36).

According to Exodus 12:6, the Jews or the assembly of the congregation of Israel, was to kill the Passover lamb "in the evening" and strike its blood on the door posts.   Jewish history records that the Passover Lamb was slain during the hours of darkness on Thursday. **Thursday was a Preparation Day** as were the other two days that were set aside for the "proving" of the lamb (Ex. 12:3). It would be good for the reader to compare these verses with those we have mentioned from Leviticus Chapters 16 and 23. It would also be prudent to remember that we will study the days of the week according to the Scripture (Genesis 1:5, 8, 13, 19, 23, and 31).

As the true Passover Lamb, Jesus was slain for our sins during hours of darkness. In Matthew 27:45 we read that "great darkness fell over the land from the sixth hour to the ninth hour.   This would have been between 12:00 noon and 3:00 P.M. according to our clock.   This darkness fell during the time that Jesus was suffering on the cross. Jesus "gave up the ghost" and finished the work of redemption on the cross about the ninth hour or about 3:00 P.M. our time (Matthew 27: 46, 50). Though I believe we can know the exact day He died, **what is truly important is that "He died for our sins" that He might redeem us.** It is important too that each of these events occurred "according to the Scripture" (I Corinthians 15:1-4). PRAISE GOD HE GAVE HIMSELF FOR US!

Pilate granted the wishes of the Jews by having Jesus and the others removed from the crosses. By doing this there would be no violation of the Jewish law or "defilement" of the high day (sabbath).

Another interesting note is that Mary went to the tomb very early in the morning on Sunday and found that Jesus had already risen (Matthew 28:1-9). There is little debate over this fact. From this it seems obvious that Jesus resurrected either, what we consider, late Saturday night or very early Sunday morning.

D. THE KEY

The key to answering the question concerning "when Christ died" seems to be to establish, with Scriptural accuracy, the day and the approximate hour in which Jesus was placed in the tomb. Once these details are established, it only remains to count forward three days and three nights to see if the time coincides with the time that Jesus resurrected according to Matthew 28:1-9.

Evidence shows that the 24 hour period that we refer to as a "day" (Monday, Tuesday... Saturday, Sunday, etc.), of the week is not the same as a "day" for the Jews. For the Jews, a "day" was a 24 hour period that began at one second after

6:00 P.M. our time and continued until 6:00 P.M., 24 hours later.   The Jews did not use 12:00 midnight as the focal point or starting point for a day as we do.   **The Jewish day** (24 hours) **began with 12 hours of darkness** (6:00 P.M. until 6:00 A.M. our time), **followed by 12 hours of light** (6:00 A.M. until 6:00 P.M.).   Remember what is said in Genesis 1:5, 8, etc., "And the **evening** *(darkness)* and the **morning** *(light)* were the **first day**."   Please refer to the chart on the last page.

SUMMARY

In summary, we are led to conclude that:

1) Jesus would have been arrested during the hours of darkness of the Jewish day, Wednesday. According to Jewish time, Wednesday would have started with 12 hours of darkness... what we call Tuesday night. This would have been sometime after 6:00 P.M. Tuesday. Remember the Jewish day begins with 12 hours of darkness (evening) and continues with 12 hours of daylight (morning).

2) Jesus would have been judged early the next morning (John 18:28). This would have been our Wednesday morning.

3) Wednesday was a "Preparation Day" Matthew 27:62), and Thursday would have been the high and holy day (high day, holy convocation or non-Saturday, sabbath).

4) Jesus was placed on the cross and remained there from noon until 3:00 P.M. on Wednesday. A great darkness came upon the earth while He hung on the cross (Matthew 27:45).

5) Jesus died at approximately 3:00 P.M. on Wednesday afternoon (Matthew 27:46, 50).

6) According to the wishes of the Jewish leaders, Jesus was removed from the cross and placed in the tomb prior to 6:00 P.M., the hour that marked the end of Wednesday (12 hours of darkness/evening and 12 hours of light), the "Preparation Day", and represented the beginning (12 hours of darkness, the evening of Genesis) of Thursday and the high and holy day, or sabbath of the Jewish Passover.

7) Jesus remained in the tomb of Joseph of Arimathea from the beginning of Thursday (what we call Wednesday night) or from 6:01 P.M. Keep in mind the fact the Jewish days were 12 hours of darkness, the **evening**, followed by 12 hours of daylight, the **morning**.

8) When Mary went to the tomb "very early Sunday morning", Jesus had already risen from the dead. Again, forgive me for belaboring the point but, according to the Jewish calendar or week, **Sunday actually began after 6:01 P.M. of what we call Saturday.** If you are familiar with the Adventist's movement you know they follow the Jewish order of the day... 12 hours of darkness followed by 12 hours of light. They stop all servile work on our Friday at sunset. They have their day of rest and worship (their Sabbath) all day Saturday and then the 7th day Sabbath/Saturday ends at 6:01 P.M. Saturday. Though we may have questions about the biblical correctness of some of their teachings, we must recognize that they know when the weekly Sabbath really begins. Jesus could have risen from the dead any time after 6:01 P.M. on what we call Saturday night and it would be according to the Jews, "Sunday." **We want to be specific: Jesus came out of the grave sometime just before Mary arrived, "very early in the morning."** For the Jews and the disciples, **Sunday morning** would have begun sometime after the 12 hours of the evening (darkness). He arose sometime after 6:01 A.M.

9) According to His own prediction or prophecy, Jesus was in the tomb (heart of the earth) for three periods of darkness (**three nights**) and three periods of light (**three days**).

25

JEWISH DAYS

Thursday	12 hours of darkness (evening)	6:01P.M. to 6:00A.M.
	12 Hours of light (morning)	6:01 A.M. to 6:00 P.M.
Friday	12 hours of darkness (evening)	6:01 P.M. to 6:00 A.M.
	12 hours of light (morning)	6:01 A.M. to 6:00 P.M.
Saturday	12 hours of darkness (evening)	6:01 P.M. to 6:00 A.M.
	12 hours of light (morning)	6:01A.M. to 6:00 P.M.

Sunday began with 12 hours of darkness (which is our Saturday night), followed by 12 hours of light (day)
(SEE THE PICTURE PAGE 28)

Without doubt, the most important thing is that Jesus died for our sins, but it is also important that our interpretation of Scripture be accurate and precise. HE died "according to the Scripture"... exactly as the Scripture predicted and states.

Jesus died for the sins of the whole world, He was buried and then the third day He came forth from the grave and is presently seated at the Father's right hand where He intercedes for those who are saved by His grace. Do you know Him as your personal savior? You may know about Him without actually knowing Him as your personal and all-sufficient Saviour.

The Scriptures teach that:

1. We are all sinners.
   *"For **all have sinned** and come short of the glory of God;..."* Romans 3:23

2. The wages (what we deserve as sinners) of sin is death.
   "For the wages of sin is death;…" Romans 6:23

3. God loves us as sinners and sent His Son to die in our place. God sent Jesus to die on the cross for my sins and yours and for those of the whole world.
   *"But **God commendeth his love toward us**, in that while we were yet sinners, **Christ died for us**.* Romans 5:8

4. If we recognize our sin and repent and place our faith (trust) in Christ, He has promised to save us and give us eternal life.
   *"For whosoever shall call upon the name of the Lord **shall be saved**."* Romans 10:13

   For God so loved the world, that he gave his only begotten Son, that whoever believeth in him should not perish, but have everlasting life. For God sent not his Son into the world to condemn the world; but that the world through him might be saved. He that believeth on him is not condemned: but he that believeth not is condemned already, because he hath not believed in the name of the only begotten Son of God."
   John 3:16-18

A DAY (ANY DAY) FOR THE JEWS BEGAN WITH 12 HOURS OF DARKNESS STARTING AT 6 PM (OUR TIME) FOLLOWED BY 12 HOURS OF LIGHT STARTING AT 6AM (OUR TIME)

GENESIS 1:5, 8, 13, 19, 23 --THE DAY BEGAN FOR THE JEWS WITH TWELVE HOURS OF DARKNESS

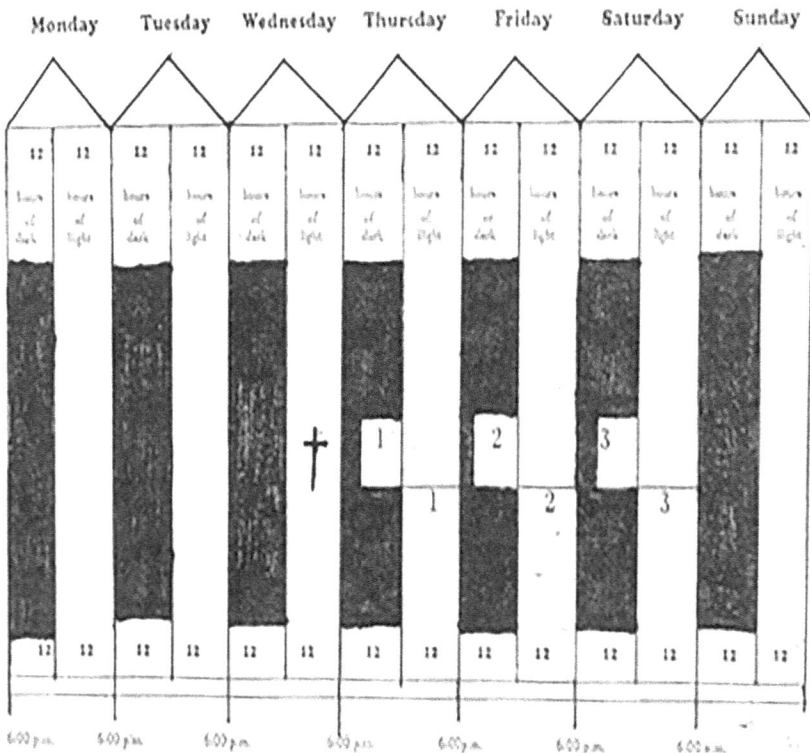

28

www.ingramcontent.com/pod-product-compliance
Lightning Source LLC
Chambersburg PA
CBHW020956030426
42339CB00005B/136